It started with...

..."I'm sorry, there's no heartbeat"

CATHY NGUYEN

BookLeaf Publishing

India | USA | UK

Presentation by *BookLeaf Publishing*

Web: www.bookleafpub.com
E-mail: info@bookleafpub.com

ISBN: 9789367393932

First edition 2025

DEDICATION

This poetry book is dedicated to my first-born daughter, Sage Azalea Wilson, who unfortunately could not stay in this world. You are the one who first made me a mother and there is not a single day I don't wish that you were here with me in person.

PREFACE

Cathy and her husband, Jacob, got married in November 2020. By early 2021, they were excited to know that they were expecting a little girl.

It was a low-risk pregnancy filled with love and innocence, and there were so many plans for the future for them all.

After nine months of pregnancy, and with the nursery room all ready, Cathy went to the hospital due to sudden changes in the baby's movement, only to receive the worst possible news a first-time mother could ever hear.

Life then completely changed when they welcomed both a lifeless baby and grief into their world.

The feeling of being robbed of the chance to ever experience parenthood without the shadow of loss and fear was very consuming, so Cathy decided to dedicate her time to advocating for pregnancy and infant loss via her words and time.

ACKNOWLEDGEMENT

I would like to acknowledge all parents who sadly have to endure this life-long grief because their child could not stay in this world. Your baby(s) will always be loved and missed.

AUTHOR BIO

Cathy has been writing poems since her teenage years as a way to express and explore emotions. Since the loss of her first-born daughter in 2021, she's immersed herself even more in her writing, using it to advocate for the emotions of loss and grief in hopes that it'd make other bereaved parents less lonely.

Cathy is also a Podiatrist and Yoga Teacher, and has also dedicated her time to providing yoga sessions for bereaved parents.

Instagram: @cathy.nguyen93

It started with...

..."I'm sorry, there's no heartbeat"

The dark clouds started to roll in above
as I awaited your silence to be assessed.
Time continues and a few more come by,
trying to hear you and see if you were simply
distressed.

My mind containing an explosion of thoughts,
of all the scenarios that could be thrown our way.
I held onto hope and the innocence of life,
that no matter what, "all would be okay."

9 months of you growing strongly within,
9 months of this special and magical connection.
9 months of seeing and feeling your dances,
9 months of beautiful love and affection.

All the plans for life I had with and for you,
all the extra love to give when we were to meet,
but sadly the universe had other plans,
and it started with...

> …*"I'm sorry, there's no heartbeat."*

How is this possible? How does this happen?
How can you no longer be alive?
Where do I go from here? What do I do?
How am I ever going to survive?

So many thoughts racing through my mind,
but the loudest one was "no, no, no."
I don't want to be here in this position,
I don't want a "goodbye" before a "hello."

Why is this happening to me? Why has this happened
to you?
These questions echoed constantly in my head.
As I feel my soul exiting my body,
I'm overcome with a dullness like I, too, am dead.

My heart is shattered into a million pieces,
a dagger forever embedded in my shell.
Preventing me from ever being whole again,
from the moment the news hit with a forced farewell.

I envisioned a labour of pure love,
of waves crashing and returning to their source.
Synchronised breaths and sways between you and me,
until the magical moment runs its course.

The beginning of your story on Earth
was not meant to start with such heartbreak.
It was meant to be only temporary surges,
not a painful void and emotional heartache.

Between the physical pain and emotional anguish,
between the bounces, stairs, showers, and sways,
between the waterfalls flowing from my eyes,
I would lay my hand on your home in loving ways.

Wishing to any higher power that the outcome is wrong,
that you are still alive, breathing inside.
That somehow, because you haven't been seen yet,
that there is still a chance I'd hear you cry.

But after nearly 30 hours of heavy-heart labour,
the moment to meet you is finally near.
And as you entered into the world sleeping and lifeless,
there were no open eyes, no cry, nothing to hear.

No amount of tears can bring you back,
no amount of broken pieces is enough to portray,
the depth of void and pain that hovers so close
knowing you cannot come home and stay.

I always thought the hardest choice
was to decide how you would enter the world,
but never in a million years and counting,
would I imagine I'd be birthing my precious and still
girl.

Having to accept not seeing you grow older,
my heart bleeds with no easing in sight.
The wound forever opened with your soul long gone,
adding to the constant, empty, and sleepless nights.

Knowing it is a permanent ticking time bomb,
to be with your physical vessel on this earth,
makes having to leave this hospital without you
hurt deeper but forever will hold its worth.

To see your body disintegrate and change
over the days of precious time together.
From bright to dull, plump to shrivelled,
adds to the never-ending guilt that stays forever.

Saying goodbye at the hospital and driving home empty
was the second moment a part of me died.
But to close the coffin and say goodbye forever,
was when I felt the death within magnified.

How cruel can nature be, to let me birth death.
For my first chest-to-chest experience to be still.
To be robbed of the chance to breastfeed,
because there was no option but to take that pill.

To go through postpartum like any other mother—
The pain, the tears, the heaviness.
But sadly alone and empty-handed,
with the loss of you: hopelessness.

Your nursery room left untouched, as it was
which can only be lived out in my dreams.
I sit here imagining what life should have been like,
and with that pain comes an inside scream.

How do I face the world as a mother?
Because the world sees me as childless.
No living baby post-birth to direct my love to,
not one chance of motherhood's happiness.

Stuck in a time when you were still here with me,
finding it difficult to step forward with such heavy feet.
Juggling both the living and the dead worlds together,
leaving me with the feeling of defeat.

There are no living children at home,
no child to pour and offer my love,
as I'm welcomed into motherhood
with loss and grief hovering above.

Alongside the loss of you
I grieve so many plans and dreams,
and in addition to the daily losses,
I'm also physically childless it seems.

Because I don't know if it'll happen,
I don't know if a sister or brother
will come along miraculously
and fill my empty arms as a mother.

There are rocks in my heart where flesh once was,
with chains attached and tangled, dragging me down.
Unable to allow even fragile steps forward,
always pulling and anchoring me to the cold ground.

There is concrete in my arteries where once was a red
flow,
but now all that remains are shades of grey.
No longer is there colour that can be seen in
abundance,
no longer does it feel like life can't get away.

How can the order be parents burying a child?
How can this foreign world make sense?
My view is upside down and cannot be turned,
not without your physical and spiritual presence.

What used to be home no longer exists,
now only emptiness resides within these walls.
And I don't know how I can keep going on,
waking up in darkness, feeling so small.

The silence everywhere is deafening and loud,
the paths ahead so chaotic and unclear,
Birthing you only to hold a funeral,
only in my dreams now can we ever be near.

Life somehow flows around me
even though my world stopped when you departed.
I'm not sure how I can ever process this,
I'm not sure how to not feel so broken-hearted.

There's loneliness in a crowd, no one can understand
the waves of turmoil pushing me under.
Numb to the cold and narrowly staying afloat,
as I fight to survive the constant thunder.

Only sleeping due to pure exhaustion,
I am lost in the ocean of my own tears.
Barely surviving the days that blur past emotionally,
and physically not even close to being in the all-clear.

I want to wake up from this horror nightmare,
I don't want this life to be my reality.
I want to see your eyes, smell you, embrace you,
I want to see you grow your personality.

I want to witness your little milestones with time,
to see you sit, crawl, stand, and walk.
To see you off on your first day of school,
and hear you learn new ways to talk.

To one day see you walk down the aisle,
if that is something you wish to do.
Or perhaps have a family of your own,
and watch you become a mother too.

I want to see you learn new skills
and be so proud of what you achieve.
To see you simply living and loving life,
but now they are all additional things I grieve.

I won't be able to see you grow,
to reach any milestones at all ages,
so secondary to the loss of you,
every day I relive grief in different stages.

There have been so many changing variables
and here I am, trying to hold on with one hand.
Dangling in the chaos of life below,
gripping so tightly without any way to stand.

My shell of glass, a tap away from breaking,
barely holding its shape externally.
And the moment I am allowed to sit with the
thoughts of you,
it shatters to reveal the ruins internally.

I don't want my only option to be strong,
I don't want to have to fight every day.
I don't want to grieve a never-ending list of losses,
I just wish you could be with me always.

All I am doing is holding on the best I can,
but I don't know what to do, I can't see a way out.
Those paved paths ahead, now in complete shambles,
since the moment I went home without.

Many nights I still cry myself to sleep
wishing this heaviness could leave with you still alive.
Dreams of living life with you in a parallel world,
where I'd look into your eyes, and you'd look into mine.

Where I could feel your breathing body on me,
as you crawl onto my chest to comfort feed.
To share that magical connection each day,
And soak up the heaven that flies by with speed.

But I open my eyes to walls of darkness,
dulled-down senses in a world of loss.
Since you're not here in reach to light it up,
the parallel world is unattainable and cannot be crossed.

I am surviving somehow, day by day,
with no destination to aim for, nothing to see.
There is no end to this grief, there is no clear way,
but scattered paths that I don't want for me.

No familiar road can be seen ahead,
none that I had previously walked along.
And out of the few steps in view,
having to choose feels so wrong.

It's scary, this unknown territory.
It's foreign, new, and petrifying.
To accept this as my new life,
and to choose a direction is terrifying.

But no matter what I do and where I go,
this heaviness follows close behind.
And when I try to move forward carefully,
it pulls me backwards at its own time.

I feel the sand around my toes,
the ground softening underneath,
as I step where the shore and the sea
dance together and meet.

I feel my body becoming lighter
as I immerse myself all in.
Surrounded by clear water,
its coolness touches my skin.

It's an overwhelming sense,
the one that wants me to stay
underneath holding my breath
until the last moment of my day.

To rid myself of this heaviness,
this gravitational force on land,
the grief that forever hovers,
that consumes me wherever I stand.

The shallow breaths,
more strenuous than before,
sucking out what energy I have left
to continue the chore.

The air surrounding me,
so thick and smothering,
slowly but surely,
making me feel the suffering.

My mind in delirium,
split into three:
A world before, during, and after,
never again to feel free.

What faith do I have left?
When betrayed by the higher powers.
Left stranded alone,
drowning in tears each hour.

How can I believe?
When all I've experienced is death.
I imagine life with my children,
but only know no breath.

What do I hold onto?
When I'm walking on a tightrope.
Always about to fall,
but somehow still trying to cope.

How can I go on?
When a part of me is absent.
And when I search for what I am now,
I'm given cycles of harsh torment.

Who am I now?
What can I do?
Try to survive?
And have hope too?

How can I drown out the external noise?
How can I block the silence at home?
No matter where I want to travel,
I am chased to the point of being alone.

I see their mouths begin to open,
I hear the lightning so sharply
as it exits and runs in my direction,
piercing my heavy heart so deeply.

Words of weight added on top,
day after day with no ease to it all.
My soul hurts from holding it up,
hoping the heaviness will soon fall.

In between days of soldiering on,
I collapse under the force of grief.
Because it's not just the death of a baby,
but other losses and cruel words with no relief.

Standing where I used to go with you,
a place of enveloped love and coolness.
So light and freeing it used to feel,
but now carries a sense of hollowness.

I feel the waves crash against me,
the turbulence pulling me in,
to drown my sorrows forever,
and have another tragedy begin.

My heart hurts thinking of this time
as we approach the end of the year.
Only this time it's not like other transitions—
no celebrations without you here.

How can I move onto a new year?
When it feels like I have to close
the chapter with all of you,
both living and dead, highs and lows.

The year your life magically began,
the year you grew and thrived,
the year I felt you dance inside,
the year you were ferociously alive.

The year things turned for the worse
when I found out you had died,
and then having to endure the long labour
to birth your body Earth-side.

The year I got to meet you
but with a broken heart and streaming tears.
Only to have to say goodbye
in many ways within the year.

All I have left is your timeline,
your memories embedded in my head,
which makes ending this year forever
another painful goodbye to dread.

These mundane tasks
repeating each morning,
sucking the energy
from what is mourning.

Covered by blankets
barely able to leave,
the fortress of grief
that imprisons the bereaved.

A bite of toast,
surely that is enough
to get through the clock
and put on a bluff.

Rained upon in the shower,
masking the tears,
sitting at the drain
dreading the years.

Every breath I take
saps the life out,
of what's left inside
of this internal drought.

So please don't judge,
please let me be.
Please don't assume,
and instead, just sit with me.

To welcome grief
is all anyone can do.
To allow for the heaviness
is the support needed to get through.

Because I will move forward,
with my grief in tow.
There will be days where I smile
and can catch what life throws.

But please be patient,
grief has its own timeline.
So until I'm ready,
having support is the lifeline.

"How are you?"
Where do I start?
"I'm shattered. I'm broken. I'm lost.
It all happened so fast.

My job as a mother ended,
I don't know why I'm still here.
I can't tend to her as planned,
and I'm left with the grief and the fear.

Everything is a blur
and I'm drowning every day.
Among the mundane tasks
that keep me going some way.

The pain is so consuming,
the hurt is too much.
All I want is her alive,
within reach to smell and touch.

I don't know how to go on,
How do I survive?
My nervous system has peaked
and is already on overdrive."

The screams of grief loudens,
ready to explode like a mine.
But as I muster up all my energy to reply,
All I manage is a whisper: *"I'm fine."*

"If only I could take away your pain,
and allow you to enjoy parenthood.
If I could make the hurt go away,
please know I'd do my best, I so would."

"I'm so sorry for your loss.
I'm so sorry she couldn't stay and be here.
I'm so sorry life is so unfair.
I'm so sorry you have to grieve for unlimited years."

"There are no words to describe the depth of pain,
no words to heal your open wounds.
No words to truly portray the void,
that remains with no baby to swoon."

"Just checking in with you,
to see how you are travelling.
Know there is no pressure to reply at all,
as I can only imagine the difficult layers unravelling."

"I don't know what to say,
I don't know how you feel.
I can only imagine what you're going through,
but know I will sit with you through the spills."

Paraphrases of what I would offer
to lessen the loneliness that surrounds.
To validate the emotions and exhaustion,
and pull the bereaved hand above ground.

But I come from a similar perspective,
living it myself from life's intersection.
A small community of bereaved parents,
that truly understand and can offer connection.

I wish they knew
how deep their knives
of harsh, cruel words
stab in this new life.

I wish they knew
how painful it feels
to hear the words, "at least"
like you aren't even real.

I wish they knew
when they tell me to be
grateful for you
it gaslights my reality.

I wish they knew
questioning my lifestyle
adds to the guilt
that already is hostile.

I wish they knew
how loneliness remains
when nothing is said
to acknowledge the pain.

I wish they knew
how my presented facade
does not show the slightest
my true emotional cards.

I wish they knew
how much energy it takes
to breathe each day
let alone communicate.

I wish they knew
how a privileged hand
can die before their child
as nature had planned.

I wish they knew
how much I try
to carry you with me
until the day I die.

After shaking hands with death
I'm unable to blend in with life.
Left to navigate alone with time
as the haunting only magnifies.

As the days turn to weeks,
as the months slowly pass by,
the loneliness becomes a companion
as everyone returns to their lives.

As much as they rightfully can,
it only heightens the difference between
the bereaved haunted by the void
and those privileged to not be seen.

My stomach churns constantly
as we approach the big milestone.
The fear of what it could be like
creeping up with all the unknown.

It feels like it was only yesterday
but now the big one year is here.
A time you should have been celebrated,
not remembered with a silent tear.

I will always wish I had at least one living day,
one day to hear you and see your eyes,
one day to hold you closely in my arms,
one day to shower you with love under the sky.

With all that I anticipate for the day
and all that I wish I could do for you,
I end up breaking down under the weight
of balancing grief with honouring you.

Out of all the things
I've been able to achieve,
simply surviving today
is a win for the bereaved.

To carry on everyday
since you've left my side,
takes tremendous strength
at a rate that multiplies.

Even though grief echoes
in my head so loud,
know that I am still living
and I hope you are proud.

I'm at a pivot point in life
where everything I know is gone.
Thrown into an unfamiliar world
and I'm forced to adapt and move on.

I dissect the path so far,
see what plans can be saved,
and think about what options I have
to continue on what was paved.

With all my might I try,
to re-route back to the main.
But with more vicious winds of life,
I'm blown off the wanted lane.

With this cycle on repeat,
only one alternative holds true,
to build a new road altogether
and try to accept what's new.

New plans on the horizon
to achieve what was envisioned.
Only now, it is turbulent
and possibly an unfulfilled mission.

All that I know of motherhood
is death, grief, and sorrow.
Days, weeks, and months of recurring events,
a void that remains so hollow.

But slowly there are moments in life
that creep towards me ever so closely.
That for others is an easy smile or laugh,
but for me is still sad mostly.

I'm not prepared for this, how do I let it in?
I don't know how to be happy anymore.
Because the sadness has connected me to you,
So any happiness feels like an internal war.

The guilt on my back from fleeting glimpses of joy
weighs heavily on me, a constant crushing form.
But as I experience lighter moments, I realise
that happiness and sadness both co-exist in grief's storm.

Your absence is always felt,
on some days more than others,
it comes in strange waves
of just breathing or feeling smothered.

One moment I am driving
then my vision suddenly blurred
as tears stream down my face
because your death has just recurred.

One moment I am walking
through the aisles at the shop
but suddenly I hear the sounds
that remind me of the way your heart stopped.

One moment I am viewing
recent photos on my phone,
when the memories quickly appear
showing your missed milestones.

One moment I am training
when I abruptly stop for a break
because your death is relived
and I cannot escape the heartbreak.

On a daily basis I try
to get my life back on track,
to continue forward with you
but grief always pulls me back.

Life has shown what truly happens,
that nothing is ever guaranteed.
That wounds opened by permanence
like death, will only continue to bleed.

And as time continues to pass by
I will grow around these wounds,
but the bleeding never ceases,
instead, the wound and progress grow in tune.

Your existence will always matter
and I'm grateful you were alive,
but it doesn't for one second lessen
the void that does not let me thrive.

I can never experience the lightness
that most mothers are privileged to feel.
In their loving journeys of matrescence
without the fear of baby loss being so real.

I envy mothers who have had the chance
to fully immerse in the joys of mothering.
To experience both highs and lows of parenthood
without the constant grief smothering.

It's easy to watch through the window and assume
but wounds do not heal with time.
So while others say they would die for their child,
I can say I will fight and live for mine.

With whatever energy there is left
I choose to offer to those who hear.
To lend a hand to soften the blows,
and really listen with both ears.

To those who choose to stay by my side
even if they cannot fully comprehend,
who will listen not to simply reply,
but to provide support as a loving friend.

It's difficult to be around people
who are so unaware otherwise.
Those who require so much explaining
and cannot naturally sympathise.

Not that others owe their time,
not that they can ever take away my pain,
but in the depths of grief from the start,
I will remember who helped or made it rain.

Many nights I visit you with tears
flowing at an unknown pace,
to hold your body, smell you close,
and truly absorb the look of your face.

I am here in this tormenting place
where you should be two and very alive,
but I can only see you in my mind's
darkest corners as I crash-dive.

My heart feels trampled just the same,
incapable of gulping what's in my throat,
nails in my limbs, and left abandoned
in the sea of sorrow unable to float.

I still can't make sense of it all
even as the years go by so quick.
Though time moves and travels on its own,
the rawness inside still feels so thick.

The plans of moving into our new house
were meant to mark a happy new start.
With you being two and a half years old in tow,
not two and a half years of being worlds apart.

The dreams of setting our forever home,
to see you grow older and play,
shattered the moment you suddenly left,
so it's difficult to move in on this day.

To say goodbye and add it to the list,
to the place where in-utero you grew.
To the place you visited after your death,
on that funeral day I somehow got through.

To close the chapter of your vessel
at a place I could no longer reach,
to a new home that is now tainted
by your absence, where misery greets.

All the mixed emotions dancing together
of wanting to leave but still holding on,
come from needing to escape the pain,
yet still carrying all memories of you along.

If you had come one day earlier into this world,
you would be by my side today, at three years old.
I always imagine what life would have been like,
had I not lost you, and grief didn't unfold.

The unanswered questions of why this is so,
of how after 9 months you couldn't come before,
because you were still beating strongly inside,
so you would have been alive and not at death's door.

It hurts to imagine all the what-ifs with you
but it's a pain that I am willing to carry and sit in
all the memories with you and emotions they hold,
to forever acknowledge you and my love within.

Life continues to unfold around
and with time, a level of joy arises.
But the guilt's shadow continues to follow,
Giving the joys different and conflicting prices.

The guilt comes from the pain and hurt
of not being able to show you the world.
Of not being able to physically raise you up,
and to see you daily as my first-born little girl.

But no matter the length of time that passes,
and no matter what level of joy sprinkles above,
it will always hurt, and it's okay for it to hurt,
because it comes from a place of misplaced love.

To my pregnant family and friends around me
who were so lucky to end up with a living child.
With the innocence of pregnancy and life intact,
and welcoming motherhood with yawns and smiles.

I'm sorry I couldn't be around more than I was,
I was barely breathing and surviving most days,
realizing how my world had come to a halt,
yet everyone else's lives continued to sway.

It made life feel so unfair and I felt left behind
to pick up my own pieces and manage the pain.
Please understand, I so wished to be a part
of the child's life and for my innocence to remain.

Please understand how difficult it then became
to see a living baby cuddled when mine died,
to be around pure happiness and joy
when so many daily events made me cry.

To feel so isolated because no one could imagine
how something in life that used to be so small,
overnight had turned into potential big triggers
that only I would protect myself from it all.

I wish life was simpler, at a time before loss,
when it would be lighter and easier to just be.
A time where play-dates and well-wishes to each other
would have been the default for everyone to see.

With the homelessness of emotions
that rain upon me each day,
the strength to survive each hour
is the power that leads the way.

It isn't something by choice
but sadly out of necessity.
The brain rewires and adapts
to remain in this world sensibly.

For this to occur to the very end,
the brain finds ways to cope.
And one of them is having me walk
the worst-case scenarios tightrope.

Because when life takes away control,
the despair is consuming and real.
But for intrusive thoughts to be familiar,
it becomes the much-needed shield of steel.

As much as I would love to feel
the lightness that life has to provide,
I would never for a moment regret
carrying and birthing you, my pride.

As much as I would love to live
without the grief and its heavy days,
I know where there is raw grief,
there is also love and will always.

You were the dream I held for years to come,
the next step in life that I was excited for.
And when it happened I was over the moon,
to welcome you with loving open doors.

I enjoyed our precious moments of two,
the connection that no one will ever know.
It's something that I will forever cherish
and will never be replaced as life flows.

I'm sorry I couldn't protect you longer,
I'm sorry your life was cruelly cut too short.
But I promise to make your life a legacy,
to honour you, and offer bereavement support.

Walking this lifelong path of unknown grief
with different branches that continue to crumble,
I am met with countless pushbacks and obstacles
but also new goals unlocked through the rumble.

It may seem that I am broken to the degree
of no longer turning at all on my clock,
but behind the tragic words that are shared,
the determination to succeed and be isn't rocked.

Grief has made it infinitely harder,
to arrive at the destination I want to reach.
And of course, it's no longer the same place or path,
but now an adjusted way no one can teach.

For what I've done in life since you've gone,
all the sacrifices and efforts I've made so far,
all the emotions I've advocated in memory of you,
I hope make you proud of me wherever you are.

Through the daily storms and thunder of grief,
and the never-ending cycles it brings.
Through the hurt and the heaviness that remains,
and the screams of pain that melancholy sings.

I step forward with one foot at a time,
balancing both worlds of *before* and *after*.
Sitting with the smiles that I allow myself,
shadowed by the sadness in my laughter.

I sometimes look back at my life and wonder how
I even made it so far from the start of grief's street.
It's all been a blur but I'm so proud of how I've moved,
and to think it all started with…

> … *"I'm sorry, there's no heartbeat."*